PRINCEWILL LAGANG

Carlos Slim: The Telecom Tycoon's Rise to Wealth and Power

First published by PRINCEWILL LAGANG 2023

Copyright © 2023 by Princewill Lagang

All rights reserved. No part of this publication may be reproduced, stored or transmitted in any form or by any means, electronic, mechanical, photocopying, recording, scanning, or otherwise without written permission from the publisher. It is illegal to copy this book, post it to a website, or distribute it by any other means without permission.

Princewill Lagang asserts the moral right to be identified as the author of this work.

First edition

This book was professionally typeset on Reedsy.
Find out more at reedsy.com

Contents

1	Introduction	1
2	A Humble Beginning	3
3	Building an Empire: Carlos Slim's Diversification Strategy	5
4	Telecom Titan: Carlos Slim's Global Ascent	7
5	Controversies and Contradictions: The Shadows of Carlos...	9
6	Legacy and Evolution: Carlos Slim in the 21st Century	11
7	The Enduring Legacy: Carlos Slim's Impact on Business and...	13
8	The Next Horizon: Carlos Slim's Enduring Influence and...	15
9	Reflections on a Legacy: Carlos Slim's Impact on Business...	17
10	Beyond the Individual: Carlos Slim's Legacy in a Changing...	19
11	Legacy in Flux: Carlos Slim's Empire in the Modern Era	21
12	Legacy Unveiled: The Enduring Lessons of Carlos Slim's...	23
13	Eternal Echoes: Carlos Slim's Legacy in the Pantheon of...	25
14	Summary	27

1

Introduction

"Carlos Slim: The Telecom Tycoon's Journey" invites readers on an insightful exploration into the remarkable life and enduring legacy of one of the most influential figures in modern business history. From the vibrant streets of Mexico City to the commanding heights of the global telecommunications industry, this narrative unveils the compelling story of Carlos Slim's ascent to wealth and power.

Chapter by chapter, we delve into the pivotal moments that defined Slim's journey—from his early entrepreneurial endeavors to the strategic diversification that laid the foundation for his vast business empire. As the narrative unfolds, readers will witness the challenges, controversies, and triumphs that marked Slim's career, providing a nuanced understanding of the man behind the telecom giant.

This exploration isn't confined to boardrooms and balance sheets; it extends into the societal impact of Slim's empire. From debates on monopolistic practices to reflections on income inequality and the ethical responsibilities of the ultra-wealthy, we navigate the complex interplay between business success and broader societal implications.

As we traverse the evolving landscapes of technology, family succession, and philanthropy, this narrative prompts reflection on the timeless lessons embedded in Slim's journey. How does one navigate the ever-changing currents of the business world? What are the ethical considerations that accompany immense wealth? And how does a legacy endure beyond the individual?

"Carlos Slim: The Telecom Tycoon's Journey" is not just a recounting of events; it's an invitation to contemplate the intricacies of entrepreneurship, the impacts of technology on global industries, and the responsibilities that come with wielding unparalleled influence. Join us on this literary expedition as we unravel the enigma of Carlos Slim, a titan whose story transcends business and reaches into the heart of contemporary discussions on success, wealth, and societal impact.

2

A Humble Beginning

In the bustling neighborhood of Mexico City, amidst the vibrant colors and sounds of the mid-20th century, a young Carlos Slim Helú began his journey—a journey that would eventually lead him to become one of the most influential figures in the global telecommunications industry. Born on January 28, 1940, into a Lebanese-Mexican family, Carlos Slim's early years were marked by modesty and a strong work ethic.

The Slim family faced its share of challenges, navigating the post-World War II era in a country striving for economic stability. Carlos, however, displayed an early aptitude for business. At the age of 11, he made his first foray into entrepreneurship by investing in government savings bonds. This small but significant step laid the foundation for the financial acumen that would later define his career.

Carlos Slim's father, Julián Slim Haddad, was a successful trader who imparted valuable lessons to his son about the importance of frugality, strategic thinking, and a long-term vision. These lessons became the cornerstones of Slim's approach to business, guiding him as he embarked on his quest for success.

As a young man, Slim pursued his studies at the National Autonomous University of Mexico, where he displayed a keen interest in engineering and economics. His academic pursuits laid the groundwork for his later endeavors in the telecommunications sector, but it was his early experiences working in his father's business that provided him with practical insights into the world of commerce.

After the passing of his father in 1953, Carlos Slim took on a more active role in managing the family's businesses. He demonstrated a remarkable ability to identify lucrative opportunities and negotiate favorable deals. These formative years instilled in him a sense of resilience and adaptability, traits that would prove indispensable in the years to come.

The landscape of Mexico in the 1960s was one of economic uncertainty and political change. Against this backdrop, Carlos Slim began making strategic investments in various industries, including construction, mining, and real estate. His diverse portfolio allowed him to weather economic downturns and position himself for future growth.

This chapter explores the early life and formative experiences that shaped Carlos Slim's character and business philosophy. From his childhood in Mexico City to his initial ventures in entrepreneurship, we witness the emergence of a young visionary who would go on to redefine the telecommunications industry and accumulate unprecedented wealth. As we delve into the intricate details of Carlos Slim's journey, we gain insights into the makings of a telecom tycoon—a man destined to leave an indelible mark on the business world.

3

Building an Empire: Carlos Slim's Diversification Strategy

With the foundation laid in the formative years of Chapter 1, we now delve into the pivotal period when Carlos Slim began to solidify his status as a business magnate. The 1970s marked a transformative era for Slim, as he strategically diversified his investments across various sectors, setting the stage for the creation of his vast business empire.

As Mexico underwent economic and political changes, Carlos Slim recognized the importance of adaptability. His visionary approach led him to explore industries beyond his initial ventures. One of the key sectors that captured his attention was real estate. Slim's shrewd investments in prime properties in Mexico City not only demonstrated his keen foresight but also laid the groundwork for future financial success.

Simultaneously, Slim ventured into the industrial and manufacturing sectors. His investments in companies involved in the production of cables, automobile components, and tobacco showcased his ability to identify emerging markets and capitalize on their potential. The diversification strategy employed by Slim was a calculated move to mitigate risks and ensure a steady stream of revenue across different economic climates.

The telecommunications industry, however, remained a focal point for Slim. As technology advanced, so did his interest in the potential of communication networks. The acquisition of the state-owned telephone company, Teléfonos de México (Telmex), in 1990 marked a watershed moment in Slim's career. This strategic move not only solidified his dominance in the Mexican telecommunications market but also positioned him as a major player on the global stage.

The chapter explores the intricacies of Slim's business acumen during this period. It analyzes his decision-making process, highlighting the calculated risks that propelled him to new heights. From negotiating high-stakes deals to leveraging political and economic changes to his advantage, Carlos Slim's ascent to wealth and power was marked by a combination of strategic vision and bold execution.

Furthermore, we delve into the challenges Slim faced during this expansion phase. Economic downturns, regulatory hurdles, and competition tested his resilience. The narrative also introduces key individuals who played crucial roles in shaping Slim's trajectory, offering readers a comprehensive view of the dynamic forces at play.

As we journey through the 1970s and 1980s, witnessing the evolution of Carlos Slim's business empire, the chapter lays the groundwork for the subsequent chapters, which will explore in greater detail the intricacies of Slim's telecommunications ventures and the impact of his empire on the global stage.

4

Telecom Titan: Carlos Slim's Global Ascent

The 1990s ushered in a new era for Carlos Slim, marked by a relentless focus on transforming the telecommunications landscape not only in Mexico but on a global scale. Chapter 3 delves into the intricate details of Slim's expansion into the telecommunications sector, exploring the strategic moves and bold decisions that solidified his position as a telecom titan.

The acquisition of Teléfonos de México (Telmex) in 1990 represented a turning point for Slim. This state-owned telecommunications giant became the cornerstone of his telecom empire. Slim's hands-on approach to management and his commitment to modernizing Telmex set a precedent for the level of innovation and efficiency he would bring to the industry.

Driven by a vision of connectivity and communication, Slim expanded his telecom holdings beyond Mexico's borders. Investments in other Latin American countries, such as Colombia and Brazil, further strengthened his regional influence. Simultaneously, he ventured into the United States market, acquiring a stake in SBC Communications (later AT&T Inc.), signaling his ambition to leave an indelible mark on the global telecommunications stage.

The chapter delves into the complexities of navigating international markets, exploring the challenges and triumphs Slim faced as he sought to establish his telecom empire beyond Mexico. Regulatory hurdles, cultural nuances, and competition on a global scale tested Slim's strategic prowess, but his ability to adapt and innovate allowed him to overcome these obstacles.

The narrative also examines the technological advancements that shaped the telecom industry during this period. The rise of the internet and the advent of mobile communication presented both challenges and opportunities. Slim's foresight in embracing these changes, coupled with strategic investments in internet infrastructure and mobile networks, positioned him at the forefront of the evolving telecommunications landscape.

As we traverse through the dynamic landscape of the 1990s and early 2000s, readers gain insights into the intricacies of Slim's telecom ventures. The chapter sets the stage for a deeper exploration of the impact of technology on his empire, the socio-economic implications of his dominance, and the controversies that accompanied his rise to power. Carlos Slim's journey from a regional telecom magnate to a global industry leader unfolds against the backdrop of a rapidly evolving digital world.

5

Controversies and Contradictions: The Shadows of Carlos Slim's Empire

As Carlos Slim's telecommunications empire reached new heights, Chapter 4 shines a spotlight on the controversies and contradictions that accompanied his rise to power. This chapter peels back the layers of Slim's business dealings, exploring the ethical and societal implications of his vast influence.

The narrative begins by examining the allegations of anti-competitive practices and monopolistic behavior that surrounded Slim's companies. Critics argued that his stranglehold on the telecommunications sector stifled competition, limiting choices for consumers and hindering economic development. We delve into the regulatory challenges and legal battles that arose as governments sought to curb his monopoly and promote fair competition.

The socio-economic impact of Slim's empire is a focal point of this chapter. While his businesses contributed significantly to Mexico's GDP and provided employment opportunities, questions were raised about the growing income inequality within the country. The concentration of wealth in the hands of one individual sparked debates about corporate social responsibility and the obligations of the ultra-wealthy to address societal issues.

Moreover, the chapter explores Slim's involvement in philanthropy and public service initiatives. While he dedicated considerable resources to various charitable causes, some critics viewed these efforts as attempts to deflect attention from the controversies surrounding his business practices. The complex interplay between Slim's business interests and his philanthropic endeavors adds layers of nuance to his public image.

The narrative also touches upon the global financial crises of the early 21st century and their impact on Slim's empire. As economic downturns shook markets worldwide, Slim faced challenges in maintaining the financial stability of his diverse portfolio. The chapter dissects the strategies he employed to navigate these turbulent times, shedding light on the resilience and adaptability that defined his business approach.

Throughout the chapter, readers gain a nuanced understanding of the man behind the empire. Carlos Slim's contradictions, from being a business tycoon to a philanthropist, from a symbol of economic growth to a target of criticism, paint a multifaceted portrait of a complex figure. The controversies surrounding his empire become a lens through which we explore broader themes of corporate power, societal impact, and the ethical responsibilities of business leaders.

As we navigate the controversies and contradictions of Carlos Slim's legacy, the chapter sets the stage for the subsequent exploration of his later years, addressing the evolving landscape of telecommunications, his family's role in his business, and the lasting imprint of his influence on the world stage.

6

Legacy and Evolution: Carlos Slim in the 21st Century

The 21st century ushered in a new phase for Carlos Slim, marked by the continued evolution of his business empire and a shifting global landscape. Chapter 5 delves into the later years of Slim's career, exploring the challenges and adaptations that defined this period, as well as the lasting legacy he crafted in the world of telecommunications and beyond.

The narrative opens with an exploration of Slim's response to the rapidly changing technological landscape. As the world became increasingly interconnected, the demand for data and mobile services skyrocketed. Slim's companies adapted by investing in cutting-edge technologies, expanding broadband infrastructure, and capitalizing on the growing prevalence of smartphones. This adaptive approach allowed Slim to maintain his relevance in an era defined by digital innovation.

The chapter also examines the role of family in Carlos Slim's business affairs. As the patriarch of a prominent family, Slim navigated the delicate balance between maintaining control of his empire and involving his children in key business decisions. The establishment of Grupo Carso as a conglomerate overseeing various business interests further underscored the family's commitment to ensuring the longevity of the Slim legacy.

In addition to his continued success in the telecommunications sector, the narrative delves into Slim's foray into other industries such as health care, infrastructure, and energy. These strategic diversifications highlighted his ability to identify emerging markets and position his companies to capitalize on new opportunities. However, they also brought new challenges and complexities, including increased scrutiny from regulators and the public.

The chapter critically examines Slim's philanthropic efforts in the 21st century. The establishment of the Carlos Slim Foundation and substantial contributions to education, healthcare, and cultural initiatives showcased a commitment to social responsibility. However, questions arose about the effectiveness of these initiatives and the extent to which they mitigated the criticisms surrounding his business practices.

As we explore the later years of Carlos Slim's career, the chapter provides a comprehensive overview of his impact on the global business landscape, his adaptive strategies in the face of technological shifts, and the evolving perception of his legacy. The narrative invites readers to reflect on the complexities of wealth, power, and influence as embodied by one of the world's most enigmatic business figures.

Chapter 5 serves as a bridge to the concluding chapters, which reflect on Carlos Slim's enduring legacy, the ongoing challenges faced by his empire, and the broader implications of his contributions to the world of business and philanthropy.

7

The Enduring Legacy: Carlos Slim's Impact on Business and Society

As we approach the final chapter of Carlos Slim's narrative, Chapter 6 delves into the enduring legacy of the telecom tycoon. This section examines the lasting impact of Slim's contributions to business, technology, and society, while also addressing the challenges and controversies that continue to shape perceptions of his empire.

The chapter begins by reflecting on the transformation of the telecommunications industry in the wake of Carlos Slim's influence. His pioneering efforts in expanding broadband access, embracing mobile technology, and navigating the digital revolution left an indelible mark on the sector. The narrative explores how Slim's innovations laid the groundwork for the interconnected world we inhabit today, shaping the way individuals communicate, work, and interact on a global scale.

Additionally, the chapter delves into the socio-economic impact of Slim's empire, both in Mexico and beyond. His businesses contributed significantly to economic growth, providing jobs and fueling development. However, questions persist about the broader societal implications of his wealth concentration and the ongoing challenges of economic inequality that transcend his era.

The narrative also addresses the evolving nature of philanthropy within the Carlos Slim Foundation and other initiatives. As his wealth continued to grow, so did the expectations placed on Slim to address pressing global issues. The effectiveness of his philanthropic efforts, the impact on the targeted communities, and the broader implications for corporate social responsibility are all scrutinized.

As the narrative unfolds, readers gain insights into Carlos Slim's later years, including any notable changes in his approach to business and his role as a global business leader. The chapter explores how he navigated the challenges of an ever-changing business landscape and the strategies employed to ensure the continued success of his empire.

Furthermore, the chapter delves into the controversies and criticisms that persisted throughout Slim's career and examines how they have shaped perceptions of his legacy. The narrative encourages readers to consider the broader implications of his business practices, the ethical dimensions of corporate power, and the lessons that can be drawn from Slim's complex journey.

Ultimately, Chapter 6 serves as a reflective conclusion to the narrative, offering readers a comprehensive understanding of Carlos Slim's impact on business, technology, and society. It invites contemplation on the multifaceted legacy of one of the world's most influential and controversial business figures, leaving readers with a nuanced perspective on the intricate interplay between wealth, power, and societal responsibility.

8

The Next Horizon: Carlos Slim's Enduring Influence and Future Perspectives

As we conclude the exploration of Carlos Slim's life and legacy, Chapter 7 looks towards the future, assessing the ongoing influence of the telecom tycoon and the potential trajectories for his empire. This chapter delves into the challenges faced by the conglomerate, the evolving landscape of global business, and the ways in which Carlos Slim's legacy continues to shape the narrative of contemporary entrepreneurship.

The narrative opens with an examination of the state of the businesses comprising Slim's empire in the present day. We explore how his telecommunications holdings have adapted to the latest technological advancements, the strategies employed to stay competitive in a rapidly evolving market, and the ways in which the conglomerate has diversified to mitigate risks.

The chapter also delves into the role of the Slim family in sustaining the legacy. With generational transitions in leadership, the narrative explores how the family navigates the delicate balance of preserving the core values and vision of Carlos Slim while adapting to the demands of an ever-changing business environment. The potential influence of new leadership and the continuity of the conglomerate's commitment to philanthropy are key focal points.

Furthermore, the narrative examines the broader implications of Carlos Slim's legacy on the business world. The chapter assesses how his successes and controversies have shaped corporate practices, regulatory frameworks, and public expectations of business leaders. Additionally, it explores the ongoing discussions around wealth concentration, corporate social responsibility, and the ethical dimensions of amassing immense fortunes.

In looking towards the future, the narrative considers the potential impact of emerging technologies, geopolitical shifts, and global economic trends on the businesses associated with Carlos Slim. The chapter also invites speculation on how his empire might continue to evolve, adapt, and potentially face new challenges.

As the story of Carlos Slim unfolds in the concluding chapter, readers are prompted to reflect on the broader implications of his legacy. The narrative encourages contemplation on the lessons that can be drawn from his life, the complexities of wealth and power, and the responsibilities of influential figures in shaping the trajectory of global business.

In conclusion, Chapter 7 serves as a bridge between the historical narrative of Carlos Slim's life and the ongoing story of his empire. It invites readers to consider the enduring influence of one of the most prominent figures in business and technology, and to ponder the ever-evolving dynamics of wealth, power, and responsibility in the contemporary business landscape.

9

Reflections on a Legacy: Carlos Slim's Impact on Business and Beyond

As we bring the comprehensive narrative of Carlos Slim's life and career to a close, Chapter 8 provides a space for reflection, allowing readers to contemplate the broader impact of Slim's legacy on the business world, society, and the ongoing discourse surrounding wealth, power, and philanthropy.

The chapter begins by revisiting key themes and milestones in Carlos Slim's journey, summarizing the triumphs, challenges, controversies, and adaptations that defined his legacy. Through a retrospective lens, readers gain a deeper understanding of the man, the empire he built, and the complexities that shaped his narrative.

The narrative then delves into the lasting imprint of Carlos Slim on the telecommunications industry. Assessing the evolution of the industry since his emergence, the chapter explores how his innovations and strategic decisions influenced the trajectory of communication technologies globally. This reflection invites readers to consider the lasting impact of Slim's contributions in shaping the interconnected world we inhabit today.

Furthermore, the chapter explores the socio-economic ramifications of Slim's business empire, both in Mexico and on the international stage. It delves into the debates surrounding wealth concentration, income inequality, and the ethical responsibilities of business leaders. Readers are prompted to reflect on the broader societal implications of extreme wealth and the role of philanthropy in mitigating social challenges.

The narrative also considers the reception of Carlos Slim's legacy by historians, business scholars, and the public. It explores the narratives that have emerged over time, the assessments of his impact on business practices, and the lessons that can be gleaned from his successes and setbacks. This section invites readers to critically engage with differing perspectives on Slim's legacy.

The chapter concludes by contemplating the enduring questions raised by Carlos Slim's journey. What can be learned from his approach to business, philanthropy, and societal impact? How has the narrative of his legacy evolved in the years since his peak influence? And what does his story reveal about the interplay between wealth, power, and the responsibilities that come with immense success?

In the final pages of the narrative, readers are encouraged to carry forward the lessons and insights garnered from Carlos Slim's life. The chapter serves as an epilogue, leaving the legacy of one of the 20th and 21st centuries' most enigmatic business figures open for ongoing exploration and interpretation.

10

Beyond the Individual: Carlos Slim's Legacy in a Changing World

As we move beyond the individual narrative of Carlos Slim, Chapter 9 shifts focus to the broader impact of his legacy in the context of a rapidly changing world. This chapter explores how Slim's influence resonates in the contemporary business landscape, technological advancements, and the ongoing discourse surrounding wealth, power, and social responsibility.

The narrative begins by examining the ripple effects of Carlos Slim's entrepreneurial journey on the next generation of business leaders. It explores how his strategies, both successful and controversial, have influenced the approaches of emerging entrepreneurs and corporate figures. The chapter assesses whether his legacy serves as a source of inspiration, caution, or a combination of both in the evolving business landscape.

Furthermore, the chapter delves into the technological advancements that have continued to shape the telecommunications industry since Slim's peak influence. The narrative explores how his early recognition of the potential in communication technologies laid the groundwork for subsequent innovations. Additionally, it reflects on how the industry has evolved in response to changing consumer behaviors, emerging technologies, and global connectivity.

In considering the broader societal impact, the chapter explores the evolving conversations around corporate social responsibility and the ethical dimensions of business practices. It assesses how the controversies and philanthropic efforts associated with Carlos Slim have contributed to ongoing discussions about the responsibilities of the ultra-wealthy and corporations in addressing societal challenges.

The narrative also addresses the international dimension of Slim's legacy, exploring how his influence has left a mark on global business practices, economic policies, and cross-border collaborations. It reflects on the ways in which his ventures beyond Mexico have shaped international perceptions of entrepreneurship, economic power, and the challenges associated with transnational business endeavors.

As the narrative unfolds, readers are prompted to consider the broader implications of Carlos Slim's legacy in the 21st century. How have his innovations and controversies influenced the trajectory of business and technology globally? What lessons can be drawn from his journey in navigating the complexities of wealth and societal impact? And how does his legacy resonate in the ongoing discourse about the role of business leaders in shaping a more equitable and sustainable world?

Chapter 9 serves as a bridge between the historical narrative of Carlos Slim's life and the ongoing conversations about business ethics, technological progress, and societal responsibility. It invites readers to contemplate the enduring impact of one of the 20th and 21st centuries' most intriguing business figures, leaving space for continued reflection on the interplay between individual success and the broader context of a changing world.

11

Legacy in Flux: Carlos Slim's Empire in the Modern Era

As we arrive at the final chapter of the narrative on Carlos Slim, Chapter 10 examines the contemporary state of his business empire and philanthropic efforts. This chapter delves into the challenges, adaptations, and innovations that define the ongoing legacy of one of the most influential figures in modern business history.

The narrative opens with an exploration of the current landscape of the businesses associated with Carlos Slim. It assesses how his telecommunications holdings and diversified investments have weathered recent economic shifts, technological advancements, and global uncertainties. The chapter provides insights into the strategies employed to maintain relevance and adapt to the demands of the ever-evolving business environment.

The role of the Slim family in steering the course of the conglomerate is a focal point of this chapter. It investigates the dynamics of generational transitions, leadership strategies, and the family's commitment to preserving the core values and vision established by Carlos Slim. The narrative also considers how new leadership may influence the trajectory of the empire.

Furthermore, the chapter explores the continued evolution of the Carlos Slim Foundation and other philanthropic initiatives. It examines how these efforts have adapted to address contemporary challenges, leveraging technology, and collaborating with global partners to make a meaningful impact in areas such as healthcare, education, and social development.

The narrative delves into the ongoing debates surrounding wealth concentration and income inequality, topics that have become increasingly prominent in public discourse. It explores how the legacy of Carlos Slim intersects with broader societal discussions about economic justice, corporate social responsibility, and the role of the ultra-wealthy in addressing pressing global issues.

In considering the future trajectory of the empire, the chapter speculates on potential areas of growth, challenges, and opportunities. It reflects on how emerging technologies, geopolitical shifts, and changing consumer behaviors may influence the businesses associated with Carlos Slim in the years to come.

Chapter 10 serves as a contemporary snapshot of Carlos Slim's legacy, offering readers a glimpse into the ongoing narrative of one of the 21st century's most impactful business figures. It invites reflection on the adaptability and resilience of his empire, the complexities of family succession in business, and the enduring questions surrounding wealth, power, and societal responsibility. As we bring this narrative to a close, readers are encouraged to consider how Carlos Slim's journey continues to shape the present and future landscape of business and philanthropy.

12

Legacy Unveiled: The Enduring Lessons of Carlos Slim's Journey

In the concluding chapter of Carlos Slim's narrative, Chapter 11 invites readers to reflect on the enduring lessons drawn from his life and legacy. This chapter distills the complexities, successes, controversies, and innovations of Slim's journey into key insights that resonate in the realms of business, technology, and societal impact.

The narrative begins by revisiting pivotal moments in Carlos Slim's story, emphasizing the transformative decisions, strategic moves, and challenges that defined his legacy. These moments serve as a foundation for the overarching lessons that emerge from his remarkable career.

One of the central themes explored is the power of adaptability. Carlos Slim's ability to navigate diverse industries, technological shifts, and economic changes highlights the importance of being agile in the face of uncertainty. Readers are encouraged to consider how adaptability can be a driving force for success in the ever-evolving landscape of business and technology.

The chapter also delves into the intricacies of wealth and power. Carlos Slim's journey prompts reflection on the responsibilities that accompany immense financial success. The narrative explores the ethical dimensions of wealth concentration, corporate social responsibility, and the ongoing discourse about the role of business leaders in addressing societal challenges.

In considering the technological impact of Slim's legacy, the narrative emphasizes the foresight to embrace innovation. His recognition of the potential in communication technologies and the strategic investments in telecom infrastructure underscore the importance of anticipating and harnessing emerging trends in a rapidly advancing digital era.

The narrative further explores the delicate interplay between business and family, shedding light on the challenges and opportunities inherent in family-led enterprises. Carlos Slim's approach to succession planning, leadership transitions, and the preservation of a family-driven legacy provides valuable insights for businesses with a familial foundation.

As the chapter unfolds, readers are prompted to consider the broader implications of Carlos Slim's journey for the next generation of entrepreneurs, business leaders, and global citizens. What enduring lessons can be gleaned from his successes and setbacks? How might his legacy inform contemporary discussions about business ethics, technological innovation, and philanthropy?

Chapter 11 serves as a reflective conclusion, offering readers a lens through which to distill the complexities of Carlos Slim's legacy into meaningful takeaways. As we bring this narrative to a close, the chapter invites readers to carry forward the lessons learned from one of the 21st century's most enigmatic business figures, encouraging continued contemplation on the ever-evolving dynamics of wealth, power, and societal impact.

13

Eternal Echoes: Carlos Slim's Legacy in the Pantheon of Business Titans

In the final chapter of the narrative on Carlos Slim, Chapter 12 considers the enduring legacy of the telecom magnate within the broader context of business history. This chapter reflects on Slim's place among the pantheon of business titans, the resonance of his legacy in contemporary discussions, and the lasting impact he has left on the global stage.

The narrative begins by positioning Carlos Slim within the continuum of influential business leaders throughout history. It explores the parallels and distinctions between Slim and other iconic figures, examining the unique attributes and contributions that distinguish him within the pantheon of business visionaries.

As the chapter unfolds, it delves into the ongoing resonance of Slim's legacy in the contemporary business landscape. How have his strategies, innovations, and controversies shaped the way business is conducted today? The narrative explores the subtle echoes of Slim's influence in the decisions of current leaders, the evolution of industries, and the ongoing discourse surrounding entrepreneurship and wealth.

Furthermore, the chapter considers the narratives and portrayals of Carlos Slim in the realms of academia, popular culture, and public perception. How has his story been interpreted, celebrated, or critiqued? The narrative invites readers to reflect on the multifaceted nature of Slim's legacy, acknowledging the diverse perspectives that contribute to the ongoing conversation about his impact.

In contemplating the lasting impact of Slim's legacy, the chapter explores the implications for future generations of entrepreneurs, business leaders, and policymakers. What lessons can be drawn from his life and career? How might his legacy inform discussions about responsible business practices, technological innovation, and the intersection of wealth and societal responsibility?

Chapter 12 serves as an epilogue, offering readers a panoramic view of Carlos Slim's legacy within the grand tapestry of business history. As the narrative concludes, it encourages readers to consider the timeless aspects of Slim's journey, acknowledging the complex interplay between individual success, societal impact, and the enduring echoes of one of the most influential business figures of the 20th and 21st centuries.

14

Summary

The narrative on Carlos Slim traces the extraordinary journey of the telecom tycoon from his humble beginnings in Mexico City to becoming one of the most influential figures in global business. The detailed exploration spans his early entrepreneurial ventures, strategic diversification into various industries, and the pivotal acquisition of Telmex that solidified his dominance in telecommunications.

Chapters unfold to reveal the challenges, controversies, and triumphs of Slim's career, examining his impact on the telecommunications sector, socio-economic landscape, and the global stage. The narrative navigates through decades of technological evolution, economic shifts, and regulatory challenges, highlighting Slim's adaptability and strategic vision.

As the story progresses, it scrutinizes the controversies surrounding Slim's empire, including allegations of monopolistic practices and income inequality. The narrative reflects on Slim's philanthropic endeavors, exploring their impact and the broader implications for corporate social responsibility.

Chapters in the later years delve into the evolving landscape of Slim's businesses, family succession, and philanthropy. The narrative considers the contemporary challenges and opportunities faced by the conglomerate, examining its adaptability to technological advancements and changing consumer behaviors.

The concluding chapters invite readers to reflect on the enduring lessons from Slim's life and legacy. Emphasizing themes of adaptability, the ethical dimensions of wealth, and the interplay between business and family, the narrative positions Slim's legacy within the broader context of business history. It prompts contemplation on his place among business titans, the ongoing resonance of his influence, and the implications for future generations.

In essence, the narrative on Carlos Slim offers a comprehensive exploration of a complex and enigmatic business figure, capturing the nuances of his journey, impact, and the timeless lessons gleaned from his life in the ever-evolving landscape of business and society.

Printed by BoD in Norderstedt, Germany